Flame and Shadow by Sara Teasdale

Sara Trevor Teasdale was born on the 8th August 1884 in St Louis, Missouri.

A woman of poor health it was only at age 10 that she was well enough to begin school when she attended the Mary Institute from 1898, but moving to Hosmer Hall from where she graduated in 1903.

Her first poem was published in William Marion Reedy's Reedy's Mirror, a local newspaper, in 1907.

Later that same year her first collection of poems, 'Sonnets to Duse and Other Poems' was published. Her well received second volume 'Helen of Troy and Other Poems', published 4 years later, was praised for its lyrical talents and subject matter.

She was courted by various men among them Vachel Lindsay, a great poet but one who thought he could not provide a suitable standard of living for her. Sara then married Ernst Filsinger, who also admired her poetry, in 1914.

Sara's third poetry collection, 'Rivers to the Sea', was published in 1915 and was a best seller. A year later, in 1916, the couple moved to New York City.

In 1917 she released her collection 'Love Songs' and the following year it won three awards: the Columbia University Poetry Society prize, the annual prize of the Poetry Society of America and, as a crowning achievement, the 1918 Pulitzer Prize for poetry

By 1929 Sara was deeply unhappy and lonely and decided to divorce. To satisfy the criteria she moved across state lines for three months. She did not wish to inform Filsinger, and only at the insistence of her lawyers, as the divorce was going through, did she—Filsinger was shocked.

After her divorce Sara remained in New York City and resumed her friendship with Vachel Lindsay, who was by this time married with children.

1931 Vachel Lindsay committed suicide.

Two year later on 29th January 1933 Sara Teasdale died from an overdose of sleeping pills. She was 48. She was buried in the Bellefontaine Cemetery in St. Louis.

Index of Contents

Flame and Shadow

I

Blue Squills

How many million Aprils came
Before I ever knew
How white a cherry bough could be,
A bed of squills, how blue!

And many a dancing April
When life is done with me,
Will lift the blue flame of the flower
And the white flame of the tree.

Oh burn me with your beauty, then,
Oh hurt me, tree and flower,
Lest in the end death try to take
Even this glistening hour.

O shaken flowers, O shimmering trees,
O sunlit white and blue,
Wound me, that I, through endless sleep,
May bear the scar of you.

Stars

Alone in the night
On a dark hill
With pines around me
Spicy and still,

And a heaven full of stars
Over my head,
White and topaz

And misty red;

Myriads with beating
Hearts of fire
That aeons
Cannot vex or tire;

Up the dome of heaven
Like a great hill,
I watch them marching
Stately and still,

And I know that I
Am honored to be
Witness
Of so much majesty.

"What Do I Care?"

What do I care, in the dreams and the languor of spring,
That my songs do not show me at all?
For they are a fragrance, and I am a flint and a fire,
I am an answer, they are only a call.

But what do I care, for love will be over so soon,
Let my heart have its say and my mind stand idly by,
For my mind is proud and strong enough to be silent,
It is my heart that makes my songs, not I.

Meadowlarks

In the silver light after a storm,
Under dripping boughs of bright new green,
I take the low path to hear the meadowlarks
Alone and high-hearted as if I were a queen.

What have I to fear in life or death
Who have known three things: the kiss in the night,
The white flying joy when a song is born,
And meadowlarks whistling in silver light.

Driftwood

My forefathers gave me
My spirit's shaken flame,
The shape of hands, the beat of heart,
The letters of my name.

But it was my lovers,
And not my sleeping sires,
Who gave the flame its changeful
And iridescent fires;

As the driftwood burning
Learned its jewelled blaze
From the sea's blue splendor
Of colored nights and days.

"I Have Loved Hours at Sea"

I have loved hours at sea, gray cities,
The fragile secret of a flower,
Music, the making of a poem
That gave me heaven for an hour;

First stars above a snowy hill,
Voices of people kindly and wise,
And the great look of love, long hidden,
Found at last in meeting eyes.

I have loved much and been loved deeply—
Oh when my spirit's fire burns low,
Leave me the darkness and the stillness,
I shall be tired and glad to go.

August Moonrise

The sun was gone, and the moon was coming
Over the blue Connecticut hills;
The west was rosy, the east was flushed,
And over my head the swallows rushed
This way and that, with changeful wills.
I heard them twitter and watched them dart
Now together and now apart
Like dark petals blown from a tree;
The maples stamped against the west

Were black and stately and full of rest,
And the hazy orange moon grew up
And slowly changed to yellow gold
While the hills were darkened, fold on fold
To a deeper blue than a flower could hold.
Down the hill I went, and then
I forgot the ways of men,
For night-scents, heady, and damp and cool
Wakened ecstasy in me
On the brink of a shining pool.

O Beauty, out of many a cup
You have made me drunk and wild
Ever since I was a child,
But when have I been sure as now
That no bitterness can bend
And no sorrow wholly bow
One who loves you to the end?
And though I must give my breath
And my laughter all to death,
And my eyes through which joy came,
And my heart, a wavering flame;
If all must leave me and go back
Along a blind and fearful track
So that you can make anew,
Fusing with intenser fire,
Something nearer your desire;
If my soul must go alone
Through a cold infinity,
Or even if it vanish, too,
Beauty, I have worshipped you.

Let this single hour atone
For the theft of all of me.

Memories

II

Places

Places I love come back to me like music,
Hush me and heal me when I am very tired;
I see the oak woods at Saxton's flaming
In a flare of crimson by the frost newly fired;
And I am thirsty for the spring in the valley

As for a kiss ungiven and long desired.

I know a bright world of snowy hills at Boonton,
A blue and white dazzling light on everything one sees,
The ice-covered branches of the hemlocks sparkle
Bending low and tinkling in the sharp thin breeze,
And iridescent crystals fall and crackle on the snow-crust
With the winter sun drawing cold blue shadows from the trees.

Violet now, in veil on veil of evening
The hills across from Cromwell grow dreamy and far;
A wood-thrush is singing soft as a viol
In the heart of the hollow where the dark pools are;
The primrose has opened her pale yellow flowers
And heaven is lighting star after star.

Places I love come back to me like music—
Mid-ocean, midnight, the waves buzz drowsily;
In the ship's deep churning the eerie phosphorescence
Is like the souls of people who were drowned at sea,
And I can hear a man's voice, speaking, hushed, insistent,
At midnight, in mid-ocean, hour on hour to me.

Old Tunes

As the waves of perfume, heliotrope, rose,
Float in the garden when no wind blows,
Come to us, go from us, whence no one knows;

So the old tunes float in my mind,
And go from me leaving no trace behind,
Like fragrance borne on the hush of the wind.

But in the instant the airs remain
I know the laughter and the pain
Of times that will not come again.

I try to catch at many a tune
Like petals of light fallen from the moon,
Broken and bright on a dark lagoon,

But they float away—for who can hold
Youth, or perfume or the moon's gold?

"Only in Sleep"

Only in sleep I see their faces,
Children I played with when I was a child,
Louise comes back with her brown hair braided,
Annie with ringlets warm and wild.

Only in sleep Time is forgotten—
What may have come to them, who can know?
Yet we played last night as long ago,
And the doll-house stood at the turn of the stair.

The years had not sharpened their smooth round faces,
I met their eyes and found them mild—
Do they, too, dream of me, I wonder,
And for them am I too a child?

Redbirds

Redbirds, redbirds,
Long and long ago,
What a honey-call you had
In hills I used to know;

Redbud, buckberry,
Wild plum-tree
And proud river sweeping
Southward to the sea,

Brown and gold in the sun
Sparkling far below,
Trailing stately round her bluffs
Where the poplars grow—

Redbirds, redbirds,
Are you singing still
As you sang one May day
On Saxton's Hill?

Sunset: St. Louis

Hushed in the smoky haze of summer sunset,
When I came home again from far-off places,
How many times I saw my western city

Dream by her river.

Then for an hour the water wore a mantle
Of tawny gold and mauve and misted turquoise
Under the tall and darkened arches bearing
Gray, high-flung bridges.

Against the sunset, water-towers and steeples
Flickered with fire up the slope to westward,
And old warehouses poured their purple shadows
Across the levee.

High over them the black train swept with thunder,
Cleaving the city, leaving far beneath it
Wharf-boats moored beside the old side-wheelers
Resting in twilight.

The Coin

Into my heart's treasury
I slipped a coin
That time cannot take
Nor a thief purloin,—
Oh better than the minting
Of a gold-crowned king
Is the safe-kept memory
Of a lovely thing.

The Voice

Atoms as old as stars,
Mutation on mutation,
Millions and millions of cells
Dividing yet still the same,
From air and changing earth,
From ancient Eastern rivers,
From turquoise tropic seas,
Unto myself I came.

My spirit like my flesh
Sprang from a thousand sources,
From cave-man, hunter and shepherd,
From Karnak, Cyprus, Rome;
The living thoughts in me

Spring from dead men and women,
Forgotten time out of mind
And many as bubbles of foam.

Here for a moment's space
Into the light out of darkness,
I come and they come with me
Finding words with my breath;
From the wisdom of many life-times
I hear them cry: "Forever
Seek for Beauty, she only
Fights with man against Death!"

III

Day and Night

In Warsaw in Poland
Half the world away,
The one I love best of all
Thought of me to-day;

I know, for I went
Winged as a bird,
In the wide flowing wind
His own voice I heard;

His arms were round me
In a ferny place,
I looked in the pool
And there was his face—

But now it is night
And the cold stars say:
"Warsaw in Poland
Is half the world away."

Compensation

I should be glad of loneliness
And hours that go on broken wings,
A thirsty body, a tired heart
And the unchanging ache of things,
If I could make a single song

As lovely and as full of light,
As hushed and brief as a falling star
On a winter night.

I Remembered

There never was a mood of mine,
Gay or heart-broken, luminous or dull,
But you could ease me of its fever
And give it back to me more beautiful.

In many another soul I broke the bread,
And drank the wine and played the happy guest,
But I was lonely, I remembered you;
The heart belongs to him who knew it best.

"Oh You Are Coming"

Oh you are coming, coming, coming,
How will hungry Time put by the hours till then?—
But why does it anger my heart to long so
For one man out of the world of men?

Oh I would live in myself only
And build my life lightly and still as a dream—
Are not my thoughts clearer than your thoughts
And colored like stones in a running stream?

Now the slow moon brightens in heaven,
The stars are ready, the night is here—
Oh why must I lose myself to love you,
My dear?

The Return

He has come, he is here,
My love has come home,
The minutes are lighter
Than flying foam,
The hours are like dancers
On gold-slippered feet,
The days are young runners

Naked and fleet—
For my love has returned,
He is home, he is here,
In the whole world no other
Is dear as my dear!

Gray Eyes

It was April when you came
The first time to me,
And my first look in your eyes
Was like my first look at the sea.

We have been together
Four Aprils now
Watching for the green
On the swaying willow bough;

Yet whenever I turn
To your gray eyes over me,
It is as though I looked
For the first time at the sea.

The Net

I made you many and many a song,
Yet never one told all you are—
It was as though a net of words
Were flung to catch a star;

It was as though I curved my hand
And dipped sea-water eagerly,
Only to find it lost the blue
Dark splendor of the sea.

The Mystery

Your eyes drink of me,
Love makes them shine,
Your eyes that lean
So close to mine.

We have long been lovers,
We know the range
Of each other's moods
And how they change;

But when we look
At each other so
Then we feel
How little we know;

The spirit eludes us,
Timid and free—
Can I ever know you
Or you know me?

In a Hospital

IV

Open Windows

Out of the window a sea of green trees
Lift their soft boughs like the arms of a dancer,
They beckon and call me, "Come out in the sun!"
But I cannot answer.

I am alone with Weakness and Pain,
Sick abed and June is going,
I cannot keep her, she hurries by
With the silver-green of her garments blowing.

Men and women pass in the street
Glad of the shining sapphire weather,
But we know more of it than they,
Pain and I together.

They are the runners in the sun,
Breathless and blinded by the race,
But we are watchers in the shade
Who speak with Wonder face to face.

The New Moon

Day, you have bruised and beaten me,

As rain beats down the bright, proud sea,
Beaten my body, bruised my soul,
Left me nothing lovely or whole—
Yet I have wrested a gift from you,
Day that dies in dusky blue:

For suddenly over the factories
I saw a moon in the cloudy seas—
A wisp of beauty all alone
In a world as hard and gray as stone—
Oh who could be bitter and want to die
When a maiden moon wakes up in the sky?

Eight O'Clock

Supper comes at five o'clock,
At six, the evening star,
My lover comes at eight o'clock—
But eight o'clock is far.

How could I bear my pain all day
Unless I watched to see
The clock-hands laboring to bring
Eight o'clock to me.

Lost Things

Oh, I could let the world go by,
Its loud new wonders and its wars,
But how will I give up the sky
When winter dusk is set with stars?

And I could let the cities go,
Their changing customs and their creeds,—
But oh, the summer rains that blow
In silver on the jewel-weeds!

Pain

Waves are the sea's white daughters,
And raindrops the children of rain,
But why for my shimmering body

Have I a mother like Pain?

Night is the mother of stars,
And wind the mother of foam—
The world is brimming with beauty,
But I must stay at home.

The Broken Field

My soul is a dark ploughed field
In the cold rain;
My soul is a broken field
Ploughed by pain.

Where grass and bending flowers
Were growing,
The field lies broken now
For another sowing.

Great Sower when you tread
My field again,
Scatter the furrows there
With better grain.

The Unseen

Death went up the hall
Unseen by every one,
Trailing twilight robes
Past the nurse and the nun.

He paused at every door
And listened to the breath
Of those who did not know
How near they were to Death.

Death went up the hall
Unseen by nurse and nun;
He passed by many a door—
But he entered one.

A Prayer

When I am dying, let me know
That I loved the blowing snow
Although it stung like whips;
That I loved all lovely things
And I tried to take their stings
With gay unembittered lips;
That I loved with all my strength,
To my soul's full depth and length,
Careless if my heart must break,
That I sang as children sing
Fitting tunes to everything,
Loving life for its own sake.

V

Spring Torrents

Will it always be like this until I am dead,
Every spring must I bear it all again
With the first red haze of the budding maple boughs,
And the first sweet-smelling rain?

Oh I am like a rock in the rising river
Where the flooded water breaks with a low call—
Like a rock that knows the cry of the waters
And cannot answer at all.

"I Know the Stars"

I know the stars by their names,
Aldebaran, Altair,
And I know the path they take
Up heaven's broad blue stair.

I know the secrets of men
By the look of their eyes,
Their gray thoughts, their strange thoughts
Have made me sad and wise.

But your eyes are dark to me
Though they seem to call and call—
I cannot tell if you love me
Or do not love me at all.

I know many things,
But the years come and go,
I shall die not knowing
The thing I long to know.

Understanding

I understood the rest too well,
And all their thoughts have come to be
Clear as grey sea-weed in the swell
Of a sunny shallow sea.

But you I never understood,
Your spirit's secret hides like gold
Sunk in a Spanish galleon
Ages ago in waters cold.

Nightfall

We will never walk again
As we used to walk at night,
Watching our shadows lengthen
Under the gold street-light
When the snow was new and white.

We will never walk again
Slowly, we two,
In spring when the park is sweet
With midnight and with dew,
And the passers-by are few.

I sit and think of it all,
And the blue June twilight dies,—
Down in the clanging square
A street-piano cries
And stars come out in the skies.

"It Is Not a Word"

It is not a word spoken,
Few words are said;

Nor even a look of the eyes
Nor a bend of the head,
But only a hush of the heart
That has too much to keep,
Only memories waking
That sleep so light a sleep.

"My Heart Is Heavy"

My heart is heavy with many a song
Like ripe fruit bearing down the tree,
But I can never give you one—
My songs do not belong to me.

Yet in the evening, in the dusk
When moths go to and fro,
In the gray hour if the fruit has fallen,
Take it, no one will know.

The Nights Remember

The days remember and the nights remember
The kingly hours that once you made so great,
Deep in my heart they lie, hidden in their splendor,
Buried like sovereigns in their robes of state.

Let them not wake again, better to lie there,
Wrapped in memories, jewelled and arrayed—
Many a ghostly king has waked from death-sleep
And found his crown stolen and his throne decayed.

"Let It Be Forgotten"

Let it be forgotten, as a flower is forgotten,
Forgotten as a fire that once was singing gold,
Let it be forgotten for ever and ever,
Time is a kind friend, he will make us old.

If anyone asks, say it was forgotten
Long and long ago,
As a flower, as a fire, as a hushed footfall
In a long forgotten snow.

VI

May Day

A delicate fabric of bird song
Floats in the air,
The smell of wet wild earth
Is everywhere.

Red small leaves of the maple
Are clenched like a hand,
Like girls at their first communion
The pear trees stand.

Oh I must pass nothing by
Without loving it much,
The raindrop try with my lips,
The grass with my touch;

For how can I be sure
I shall see again
The world on the first of May
Shining after the rain?

"Since There Is No Escape"

Since there is no escape, since at the end
My body will be utterly destroyed,
This hand I love as I have loved a friend,
This body I tended, wept with and enjoyed;
Since there is no escape even for me
Who love life with a love too sharp to bear:
The scent of orchards in the rain, the sea
And hours alone too still and sure for prayer—
Since darkness waits for me, then all the more
Let me go down as waves sweep to the shore
In pride; and let me sing with my last breath;
In these few hours of light I lift my head;
Life is my lover—I shall leave the dead
If there is any way to baffle death.

"The Dreams of My Heart"

The dreams of my heart and my mind pass,
Nothing stays with me long,
But I have had from a child
The deep solace of song;

If that should ever leave me,
Let me find death and stay
With things whose tunes are played out and forgotten
Like the rain of yesterday.

"A Little While"

A little while when I am gone
My life will live in music after me,
As spun foam lifted and borne on
After the wave is lost in the full sea.

A while these nights and days will burn
In song with the bright frailty of foam,
Living in light before they turn
Back to the nothingness that is their home.

The Garden

My heart is a garden tired with autumn,
Heaped with bending asters and dahlias heavy and dark,
In the hazy sunshine, the garden remembers April,
The drench of rains and a snow-drop quick and clear as a spark;

Daffodils blowing in the cold wind of morning,
And golden tulips, goblets holding the rain—
The garden will be hushed with snow, forgotten soon, forgotten—
After the stillness, will spring come again?

The Wine

I cannot die, who drank delight
From the cup of the crescent moon,

And hungrily as men eat bread,
Loved the scented nights of June.

The rest may die—but is there not
Some shining strange escape for me
Who sought in Beauty the bright wine
Of immortality?

In a Cuban Garden

Hibiscus flowers are cups of fire,
(Love me, my lover, life will not stay)
The bright poinsettia shakes in the wind,
A scarlet leaf is blowing away.

A lizard lifts his head and listens—
Kiss me before the noon goes by,
Here in the shade of the ceiba hide me
From the great black vulture circling the sky.

"If I Must Go"

If I must go to heaven's end
Climbing the ages like a stair,
Be near me and forever bend
With the same eyes above me there;
Time will fly past us like leaves flying,
We shall not heed, for we shall be
Beyond living, beyond dying,
Knowing and known unchangeably.

VII

In Spring, Santa Barbara

I have been happy two weeks together,
My love is coming home to me,
Gold and silver is the weather
And smooth as lapis is the sea.

The earth has turned its brown to green
After three nights of humming rain,

And in the valleys peck and preen
Linnets with a scarlet stain.

High in the mountains all alone
The wild swans whistle on the lakes,
But I have been as still as stone,
My heart sings only when it breaks.

White Fog

Heaven-invading hills are drowned
In wide moving waves of mist,
Phlox before my door are wound
In dripping wreaths of amethyst.

Ten feet away the solid earth
Changes into melting cloud,
There is a hush of pain and mirth,
No bird has heart to speak aloud.

Here in a world without a sky,
Without the ground, without the sea,
The one unchanging thing is I,
Myself remains to comfort me.

Arcturus

Arcturus brings the spring back
As surely now as when
He rose on eastern islands
For Grecian girls and men;

The twilight is as clear a blue,
The star as shaken and as bright,
And the same thought he gave to them
He gives to me to-night.

Moonlight

It will not hurt me when I am old,
A running tide where moonlight burned
Will not sting me like silver snakes;

The years will make me sad and cold,
It is the happy heart that breaks.

The heart asks more than life can give,
When that is learned, then all is learned;
The waves break fold on jewelled fold,
But beauty itself is fugitive,
It will not hurt me when I am old.

Morning Song

A diamond of a morning
Waked me an hour too soon;
Dawn had taken in the stars
And left the faint white moon.

O white moon, you are lonely,
It is the same with me,
But we have the world to roam over,
Only the lonely are free.

Gray Fog

A fog drifts in, the heavy laden
Cold white ghost of the sea—
One by one the hills go out,
The road and the pepper-tree.

I watch the fog float in at the window
With the whole world gone blind,
Everything, even my longing, drowses,
Even the thoughts in my mind.

I put my head on my hands before me,
There is nothing left to be done or said,
There is nothing to hope for, I am tired,
And heavy as the dead.

Bells

At six o'clock of an autumn dusk
With the sky in the west a rusty red,

The bells of the mission down in the valley
Cry out that the day is dead.

The first star pricks as sharp as steel—
Why am I suddenly so cold?
Three bells, each with a separate sound
Clang in the valley, wearily tolled.

Bells in Venice, bells at sea,
Bells in the valley heavy and slow—
There is no place over the crowded world
Where I can forget that the days go.

Lovely Chance

O lovely chance, what can I do
To give my gratefulness to you?
You rise between myself and me
With a wise persistency;
I would have broken body and soul,
But by your grace, still I am whole.
Many a thing you did to save me,
Many a holy gift you gave me,
Music and friends and happy love
More than my dearest dreaming of;
And now in this wide twilight hour
With earth and heaven a dark, blue flower,
In a humble mood I bless
Your wisdom—and your waywardness.
You brought me even here, where I
Live on a hill against the sky
And look on mountains and the sea
And a thin white moon in the pepper tree.

VIII

"There Will Come Soft Rains"

(War Time)

There will come soft rains and the smell of the ground,
And swallows circling with their shimmering sound;

And frogs in the pools singing at night,

And wild plum-trees in tremulous white;

Robins will wear their feathery fire
Whistling their whims on a low fence-wire;

And not one will know of the war, not one
Will care at last when it is done.

Not one would mind, neither bird nor tree
If mankind perished utterly;

And Spring herself, when she woke at dawn,
Would scarcely know that we were gone.

In a Garden

The world is resting without sound or motion,
Behind the apple tree the sun goes down
Painting with fire the spires and the windows
In the elm-shaded town.

Beyond the calm Connecticut the hills lie
Silvered with haze as fruits still fresh with bloom,
The swallows weave in flight across the zenith
On an aerial loom.

Into the garden peace comes back with twilight,
Peace that since noon had left the purple phlox,
The heavy-headed asters, the late roses
And swaying hollyhocks.

For at high-noon I heard from this same garden
The far-off murmur as when many come;
Up from the village surged the blind and beating
Red music of a drum;

And the hysterical sharp fife that shattered
The brittle autumn air,
While they came, the young men marching
Past the village square. . . .

Across the calm Connecticut the hills change
To violet, the veils of dusk are deep—
Earth takes her children's many sorrows calmly
And stills herself to sleep.

Nahant

Bowed as an elm under the weight of its beauty,
So earth is bowed, under her weight of splendor,
Molten sea, richness of leaves and the burnished
Bronze of sea-grasses.

Clefts in the cliff shelter the purple sand-peas
And chicory flowers bluer than the ocean
Flinging its foam high, white fire in sunshine,
Jewels of water.

Joyous thunder of blown waves on the ledges,
Make me forget war and the dark war-sorrow—
Against the sky a sentry paces the sea-cliff
Slim in his khaki.

Winter Stars

I went out at night alone;
The young blood flowing beyond the sea
Seemed to have drenched my spirit's wings—
I bore my sorrow heavily.

But when I lifted up my head
From shadows shaken on the snow,
I saw Orion in the east
Burn steadily as long ago.

From windows in my father's house,
Dreaming my dreams on winter nights,
I watched Orion as a girl
Above another city's lights.

Years go, dreams go, and youth goes too,
The world's heart breaks beneath its wars,
All things are changed, save in the east
The faithful beauty of the stars.

A Boy

Out of the noise of tired people working,

Harried with thoughts of war and lists of dead,
His beauty met me like a fresh wind blowing,
Clean boyish beauty and high-held head.

Eyes that told secrets, lips that would not tell them,
Fearless and shy the young unwearied eyes—
Men die by millions now, because God blunders,
Yet to have made this boy he must be wise.

Winter Dusk

I watch the great clear twilight
Veiling the ice-bowed trees;
Their branches tinkle faintly
With crystal melodies.

The larches bend their silver
Over the hush of snow;
One star is lighted in the west,
Two in the zenith glow.

For a moment I have forgotten
Wars and women who mourn—
I think of the mother who bore me
And thank her that I was born.

By the Sea

IX

The Unchanging

Sun-swept beaches with a light wind blowing
From the immense blue circle of the sea,
And the soft thunder where long waves whiten—
These were the same for Sappho as for me.

Two thousand years—much has gone by forever,
Change takes the gods and ships and speech of men—
But here on the beaches that time passes over
The heart aches now as then.

June Night

Oh Earth, you are too dear to-night,
How can I sleep while all around
Floats rainy fragrance and the far
Deep voice of the ocean that talks to the ground?

Oh Earth, you gave me all I have,
I love you, I love you,—oh what have I
That I can give you in return—
Except my body after I die?

"Like Barley Bending"

Like barley bending
In low fields by the sea,
Singing in hard wind
Ceaselessly;

Like barley bending
And rising again,
So would I, unbroken,
Rise from pain;

So would I softly,
Day long, night long,
Change my sorrow
Into song.

"Oh Day of Fire and Sun"

Oh day of fire and sun,
Pure as a naked flame,
Blue sea, blue sky and dun
Sands where he spoke my name;

Laughter and hearts so high
That the spirit flew off free,
Lifting into the sky
Diving into the sea;

Oh day of fire and sun
Like a crystal burning,
Slow days go one by one,

But you have no returning.

"I Thought of You"

I thought of you and how you love this beauty,
And walking up the long beach all alone
I heard the waves breaking in measured thunder
As you and I once heard their monotone.

Around me were the echoing dunes, beyond me
The cold and sparkling silver of the sea—
We two will pass through death and ages lengthen
Before you hear that sound again with me.

On the Dunes

If there is any life when death is over,
These tawny beaches will know much of me,
I shall come back, as constant and as changeful
As the unchanging, many-colored sea.

If life was small, if it has made me scornful,
Forgive me; I shall straighten like a flame
In the great calm of death, and if you want me
Stand on the sea-ward dunes and call my name.

Spray

I knew you thought of me all night,
I knew, though you were far away;
I felt your love blow over me
As if a dark wind-riven sea
Drenched me with quivering spray.

There are so many ways to love
And each way has its own delight—
Then be content to come to me
Only as spray the beating sea
Drives inland through the night.

If Death Is Kind

Perhaps if Death is kind, and there can be returning,
We will come back to earth some fragrant night,
And take these lanes to find the sea, and bending
Breathe the same honeysuckle, low and white.

We will come down at night to these resounding beaches
And the long gentle thunder of the sea,
Here for a single hour in the wide starlight
We shall be happy, for the dead are free.

X

Thoughts

When I am all alone
Envy me most,
Then my thoughts flutter round me
In a glimmering host;

Some dressed in silver,
Some dressed in white,
Each like a taper
Blossoming light;

Most of them merry,
Some of them grave,
Each of them lithe
As willows that wave;

Some bearing violets,
Some bearing bay,
One with a burning rose
Hidden away—

When I am all alone
Envy me then,
For I have better friends
Than women and men.

Faces

People that I meet and pass

In the city's broken roar,
Faces that I lose so soon
And have never found before,

Do you know how much you tell
In the meeting of our eyes,
How ashamed I am, and sad
To have pierced your poor disguise?

Secrets rushing without sound
Crying from your hiding places—
Let me go, I cannot bear
The sorrow of the passing faces.

—People in the restless street,
Can it be, oh can it be
In the meeting of our eyes
That you know as much of me?

Evening: New York

Blue dust of evening over my city,
Over the ocean of roofs and the tall towers
Where the window-lights, myriads and myriads,
Bloom from the walls like climbing flowers.

Snowfall

"She can't be unhappy," you said,
"The smiles are like stars in her eyes,
And her laugh is thistledown
Around her low replies."
"Is she unhappy?" you said—
But who has ever known
Another's heartbreak—
All he can know is his own;
And she seems hushed to me,
As hushed as though
Her heart were a hunter's fire
Smothered in snow.

The Silent Battle

(In Memory of J. W. T. Jr.)

He was a soldier in that fight
Where there is neither flag nor drum,
And without sound of musketry
The stealthy foemen come.

Year in, year out, by day and night
They forced him to a slow retreat,
And for his gallant fight alone
No fife was blown, and no drum beat.

In winter fog, in gathering mist
The gray grim battle had its end—
And at the very last we knew
His enemy had turned his friend.

The Sanctuary

If I could keep my innermost Me
Fearless, aloof and free
Of the least breath of love or hate,
And not disconsolate
At the sick load of sorrow laid on men;
If I could keep a sanctuary there
Free even of prayer,
If I could do this, then,
With quiet candor as I grew more wise
I could look even at God with grave forgiving eyes.

At Sea

In the pull of the wind I stand, lonely,
On the deck of a ship, rising, falling,
Wild night around me, wild water under me,
Whipped by the storm, screaming and calling.

Earth is hostile and the sea hostile,
Why do I look for a place to rest?
I must fight always and die fighting
With fear an unhealing wound in my breast.

Dust

When I went to look at what had long been hidden,
A jewel laid long ago in a secret place,
I trembled, for I thought to see its dark deep fire—
But only a pinch of dust blew up in my face.

I almost gave my life long ago for a thing
That has gone to dust now, stinging my eyes—
It is strange how often a heart must be broken
Before the years can make it wise.

The Long Hill

I must have passed the crest a while ago
And now I am going down—
Strange to have crossed the crest and not to know,
But the brambles were always catching the hem of my gown.

All the morning I thought how proud I should be
To stand there straight as a queen,
Wrapped in the wind and the sun with the world under me—
But the air was dull, there was little I could have seen.

It was nearly level along the beaten track
And the brambles caught in my gown—
But it's no use now to think of turning back,
The rest of the way will be only going down.

XI

Summer Storm

The panther wind
Leaps out of the night,
The snake of lightning
Is twisting and white,
The lion of thunder
Roars—and we
Sit still and content
Under a tree—
We have met fate together
And love and pain,

Why should we fear
The wrath of the rain!

In the End

All that could never be said,
All that could never be done,
Wait for us at last
Somewhere back of the sun;

All the heart broke to forego
Shall be ours without pain,
We shall take them as lightly as girls
Pluck flowers after rain.

And when they are ours in the end
Perhaps after all
The skies will not open for us
Nor heaven be there at our call.

"It Will Not Change"

It will not change now
After so many years;
Life has not broken it
With parting or tears;
Death will not alter it,
It will live on
In all my songs for you
When I am gone.

Change

Remember me as I was then;
Turn from me now, but always see
The laughing shadowy girl who stood
At midnight by the flowering tree,
With eyes that love had made as bright
As the trembling stars of the summer night.

Turn from me now, but always hear
The muted laughter in the dew

Of that one year of youth we had,
The only youth we ever knew—
Turn from me now, or you will see
What other years have done to me.

Water Lilies

If you have forgotten water lilies floating
On a dark lake among mountains in the afternoon shade,
If you have forgotten their wet, sleepy fragrance,
Then you can return and not be afraid.

But if you remember, then turn away forever
To the plains and the prairies where pools are far apart,
There you will not come at dusk on closing water lilies,
And the shadow of mountains will not fall on your heart.

"Did You Never Know?"

Did you never know, long ago, how much you loved me—
That your love would never lessen and never go?
You were young then, proud and fresh-hearted,
You were too young to know.

Fate is a wind, and red leaves fly before it
Far apart, far away in the gusty time of year—
Seldom we meet now, but when I hear you speaking,
I know your secret, my dear, my dear.

The Treasure

When they see my songs
They will sigh and say,
"Poor soul, wistful soul,
Lonely night and day."

They will never know
All your love for me
Surer than the spring,
Stronger than the sea;

Hidden out of sight

Like a miser's gold
In forsaken fields
Where the wind is cold.

The Storm

I thought of you when I was wakened
By a wind that made me glad and afraid
Of the rushing, pouring sound of the sea
That the great trees made.

One thought in my mind went over and over
While the darkness shook and the leaves were thinned—
I thought it was you who had come to find me,
You were the wind.

Songs For Myself

XII

The Tree

Oh to be free of myself,
With nothing left to remember,
To have my heart as bare
As a tree in December;

Resting, as a tree rests
After its leaves are gone,
Waiting no more for a rain at night
Nor for the red at dawn;

But still, oh so still
While the winds come and go,
With no more fear of the hard frost
Or the bright burden of snow;

And heedless, heedless
If anyone pass and see
On the white page of the sky
Its thin black tracery.

At Midnight

Now at last I have come to see what life is,
Nothing is ever ended, everything only begun,
And the brave victories that seem so splendid
Are never really won.

Even love that I built my spirit's house for,
Comes like a brooding and a baffled guest,
And music and men's praise and even laughter
Are not so good as rest.

Song Making

My heart cried like a beaten child
Ceaselessly all night long;
I had to take my own cries
And thread them into a song.

One was a cry at black midnight
And one when the first cock crew—
My heart was like a beaten child,
But no one ever knew.

Life, you have put me in your debt
And I must serve you long—
But oh, the debt is terrible
That must be paid in song.

Alone

I am alone, in spite of love,
In spite of all I take and give—
In spite of all your tenderness,
Sometimes I am not glad to live.

I am alone, as though I stood
On the highest peak of the tired gray world,
About me only swirling snow,
Above me, endless space unfurled;

With earth hidden and heaven hidden,
And only my own spirit's pride
To keep me from the peace of those

Who are not lonely, having died.

Red Maples

In the last year I have learned
How few men are worth my trust;
I have seen the friend I loved
Struck by death into the dust,
And fears I never knew before
Have knocked and knocked upon my door—
"I shall hope little and ask for less,"
I said, "There is no happiness."

I have grown wise at last—but how
Can I hide the gleam on the willow-bough,
Or keep the fragrance out of the rain
Now that April is here again?
When maples stand in a haze of fire
What can I say to the old desire,
What shall I do with the joy in me
That is born out of agony?

Debtor

So long as my spirit still
Is glad of breath
And lifts its plumes of pride
In the dark face of death;
While I am curious still
Of love and fame,
Keeping my heart too high
For the years to tame,
How can I quarrel with fate
Since I can see
I am a debtor to life,
Not life to me?

The Wind in the Hemlock

Steely stars and moon of brass,
How mockingly you watch me pass!
You know as well as I how soon

I shall be blind to stars and moon,
Deaf to the wind in the hemlock tree,
Dumb when the brown earth weighs on me.

With envious dark rage I bear,
Stars, your cold complacent stare;
Heart-broken in my hate look up,
Moon, at your clear immortal cup,
Changing to gold from dusky red—
Age after age when I am dead
To be filled up with light, and then
Emptied, to be refilled again.

What has man done that only he
Is slave to death—so brutally
Beaten back into the earth
Impatient for him since his birth?

Oh let me shut my eyes, close out
The sight of stars and earth and be
Sheltered a minute by this tree.
Hemlock, through your fragrant boughs
There moves no anger and no doubt,
No envy of immortal things.
The night-wind murmurs of the sea
With veiled music ceaselessly,
That to my shaken spirit sings.
From their frail nest the robins rouse,
In your pungent darkness stirred,
Twittering a low drowsy word—
And me you shelter, even me.
In your quietness you house
The wind, the woman and the bird.
You speak to me and I have heard:

If I am peaceful, I shall see
Beauty's face continually;
Feeding on her wine and bread
I shall be wholly comforted,
For she can make one day for me
Rich as my lost eternity.

Sara Teasdale – A Concise Bibliography

Sonnets to Duse & Other Poems (1907)
Helen of Troy & Other Poems (1911)

Rivers to the Sea (1915)
Love Songs (1917)
Barter (1918)
Flame and Shadow (1920)
Dark of the Moon (1926)
Stars To-night (1930)
Strange Victory (1933)

www.ingramcontent.com/pod-product-compliance
Lightning Source LLC
Chambersburg PA
CBHW070117070426
42448CB00040B/3121